## Other Titles by Sara June Woods

Sara or the Existence of Fire by Sara Woods

Sea-Witch v.1 May She Lay Us Waste by Moss Angel Witchmonstr

Sea-Witch v.2 Girldirt Angelfog by Moss Angel the Undying

Sea-Witch v.3 Mare Piss Superkill by Møss Høpe Ångel

Careful Mountain by Sara June Woods
Cover & interior design by Sara June Woods
Second Edition, 2018 Oh! Map Books
First Edition, 2016 CCM

ISBN - 978-1-937865-65-8

# CAREFUL MOUNTAIN

*by*

# SARA JUNE WOODS

*Earlier versions of select pieces appeared previously in Guernica, 22nd Century Literature, Potluck Magazine, TheNewerYork, Sundog Lit and in the chapbooks Speckled Flowers (Persistent Editions 2013), Warm Morning (The New Megaphone, 2014) and Don't Smoke in Bed (Saucepot Press, 2015).*

*for Irene*

i. - viii.

# SPECKLED

# FLOWERS

*I keep waking up to lakes.*
There is a lake in our crawl space
& one in the yard.
Our 3 cats are all lakes now.
I stopped going to work
because my job became a lake.

You are, as of this morning, a lake
that brought me speckled flowers
as an apology for letting loose
that gleaming thing we will
for now call a demon,
who eats speckled flowers,
& draws pictures of
the most terrible things
we keep hanging in the kitchen.

I like swimming in you.
I want to push a deer into you.
I want to call her parents all distraught
but it's long distance
& I used all my money buying
endangered species stamps.

Dear Congressman,
I applaud you for your stance
on the demon bill, but I question
the effectiveness of your lake proposition.
Our children are beautiful & enjoying
their lives in the circus. I gave them
matching bowl cuts & demonproof
vests to wear. Please come home.

We miss the stories you tell
about crying on beaches.
Your loving wife,
Sara.

P.S. Attached are drugs.
We live in a world with drugs.
& so I included some of them.

P.P.S When you come home I will
show you the beautiful lizards
populating our home's many lakes
& how they sun themselves on rocks
& how they feel sorry for us
& our warm blood
& our cold hands
& our loud nights
& our mumbled apologies
to the neighbors in the morning.

careful mtn by sour june monstr

To My Dearest Whom-it-May-Concern,

I am very interested in
the position you posted.
The one where you said
you were looking for a lake
with strong communication skills,
with experience planning
events with some level of
emotional conflict.

I am not yet a lake,
though I should note
both my hands are lakes
of deer-blessed holy water
with golden-sand beaches
& 900 drunk lifeguards
with faces like burnt wood.
I do have experience planning
such complicated events.

Our wedding was beautiful,
with all its speckled flowers.
All the people were dressed up
like deer & all the deer were dressed up
like box elders & all the box elders were dressed up
like people & all our feelings were dressed up
like the feelings of the people
we wished we were instead.

It was officiated by a magnificent lake,
whose words were dressed up like
whole families so small you could
hold them under your tongue
to help you sleep at night.

Dearest Whom-it-May, I don't know
if this sounds familiar, but it should.
You were there. I remember.
Because I stretched my arms around you
& you stretched your arms around me

speckld flours

& I said congressman you are doing fine work.
Fine, fine work for our great country.

& the magnificent lake
made sounds like more families,
& I voted for your reelection
& you voted for my reelection
& you made the sounds
of a lake filled with swimmers
who could no longer find one another.

Now I have spent all my money
on magnificent lizards
whom I have trained
to carve sympathetic,
concerned expressions
on the face of the large
me-shaped boulder
I sent you after I left.

Which now sits in our home
next to the large
congressman-shaped boulder
you sent me after you left
that wears a fire-colored necktie delicately
embroidered with the words
~who is paying our rent~

& so I hope you will consider me
for this position, as I have such high hopes
& only a low-grade fever.
The lowest fever I have had
in a very long time.

Professionally yours forever,
Sara

careful mtn by sour june monstr

Congressman, O, Congressman!
I have been working on a play about you.
It features a 10-story cardboard
monument with real glass windows
that collapses as soon as the curtains part,
right onto the audience,
who are loving this,
& shout more! more!
Some of them are bloody,
& the ones who are not bloody
are screaming we're not bloody yet.
& so the rest of the play is everyone
on the cast & crew building another one,
another congressional monument,
from the scraps of the old one
& some new cardboard & glass
we have to have shipped in
on short notice,
& the audience's
patience is dwindling.
Meanwhile you are backstage,
as we are dousing the second
monument in kerosene
asking yourself
how is this about me?

Dear bright March,
Dear last parking
lot snow mountain,

You are a tiny lake
without a hole to sit in.
Someday we will marry.
Someday our beautiful rain-
haired children will play on you
while we stand by, blowing into our fists.
I could give you a medal.
You could be a pony on a beach.

I have 3 speckled flowers
in a vase you gave me.
Looking at them makes me feel
like a pony on a beach.
I put them by the window,
so they could see the sun,
& make decisions about how (& if)
they want to grow from here.
The same way we're always doing.

Dear lakes, you're deeper
& softer at the bottom
than ever before.
I learned this from a TV ad
with 1000 Pembroke Corgis
in a field of blackcurrant berries
& 12 suns in the sky
rising & setting in fast motion
& an announcer letting me know
that you're deeper & softer
at the bottom than ever before

& it's true!
I can feel it with my toes.
Somehow there are 10 of you
in me drawing pictures
of dogs in detailed pencil.
I swear their fur moves

when I open the fridge door
where I have hung them.
This makes me feel
like a pony on a beach,
abandoned by her parents,
who thought she got a ride home
with the congressman's parents
who sometimes sing at church.

Dear church rafters,
dear choir, dear songs sung
at the midday wakes held
for our fire-colored lizards
& their fire-colored drapes
in their fire-colored rental properties.
We drained all our lakes
in the memory of the time
we petted your skin
& felt all your toothpick bones,
like ponies on beaches,
moving gently underneath.

Dear sun, dear thunder,
I have spent all my money on a field,
lawnmowers & gasoline so I might write
these words large enough for you to read them.
This field will later become our home
once you finish your coursework
on warm sunbeams shining through glass
& it becomes very fashionable to live in fields.

Dear thunder, dear sun,
you are sewing me a beautiful hat
the color of speckled flowers.
I will wear it for years
& give it to a young girl
who will someday grow up
to be a lake her family can swim in.
They will cheer & buy a boat,
& no one will care about my hat.

I saw an ant carrying
a dead ant I had killed,
he could barely take it,
& paced in slow, irregular circles.
Ant, where are you going?
Ant, you are a lake I am on the beaches of.
Ant, you & I are mountains covered in snow
that don't go to church.
Instead we make our own
out of the bones of old demons
who nibbled our ears & necks & tunelessly
sang I Can Never Go Home Anymore,
who once sunned their gleaming
selves on the rocks of our beaches.

Drunk thunder! Drunk sun!
We are a confused, sleepy people
who thought a demon of a
meteor that crashed here,
leaving us this crater & now we sit,
watching the sky fumble with the light
switch in this warm dirt.
I am the lake of you.

careful mtn by sour june monstr

Dear sky-deer cloud thing,
you are a girl born of the fire
the congressman has lobbied for.
I am a girl born of a series of lakes,
a list of lakes I am adding your name to.
My hands are all lizards, singing &
laughing in you. You are my parents'
front yard. Their VCR. The plates in
their kitchen. All of their carpet.

Here is a letter I wrote you:

Dear amber morning,
I received your letter, but
when I opened the envelope all
that came out was winter.
It has taken me months to get rid
of this winter, but I can see that it was
marvelous in retrospect. The lizards
have all died, & I miss them.
They were soft machines built for
your heat. I have all your children
here & they asked me to tell
you that they have all won gold
medals in the Olympics they made up
for sports played on & around couches.

Amber sky cloud morning deer-color thing!
Are you here? Could you come back?
I have written down 10000
words I need to whisper into your hair!
I imagine they will make it strong & healthy,
& you will be able to get work
starring in shampoo commercials.

We are these lakes together.
We are clouds still on fire together
from our fire-colored field trip,
where we put our arms in boxes,
where we put our lakes in cubbies
& went pushing the sun against the sky.

~~Sara

Demon, you snow-drinker,
You are dangerous & uncareful!
When I open my front door
the stems of 10000 speckled
flowers avalanche onto my legs.

I should have never let you in
to make a phone call when
your imaginary car ran out
of imaginary gas.
When I could have given you
the imaginary gas I keep
in the crawl space
& am always smelling there
in the dark that hangs out
in that particular house-spot.

Instead I gave you quarters
I pulled from your ear
one after another,
each harder to pull than the last.

When I finished,
your ear was bloody
& you were crying.
Demon, I should
have stopped sooner.

careful mtn by sour june monstr

Dear bright morning,

You stole me, I like that.
You are a big healthy sun
in a deer-colored sky
& I am keeping all my favorite
things in my pockets.
This airport is a church
to the sky & you are the sky.
Services are open to all
early risers, we will take
you to a higher plane.
The choir are all lizards,
like you'd guess. You gave them
3 coins for their singing
& a damp cloth that
feels like their mother's
tongue. I invited 3 lizards
home & made them beds
& cooked them so much soup
they will never get sick again.

Congressman! Go home,
you are drunk. He tells me no.
He tells me well, yes, he is drunk,
but he cannot go home because
his home is dark & cold
& full of silverfish & earwigs
& other things that would be
less terrifying if they had wings.

Let me tell you, bright m,
I had wings, but my wings are now
lakes, & all the water falls out
when I use them. You have wings
but your wings got too good:
a lil flutter & you're on the moon
& I miss you more than anything.

I have spent all my money,
but I have spent it well, on nothing,

which was my plan because
now when we are alone we
know for a fact no
presidents are listening.
It is only in a safe space such
as this one I can tell you
about the black ops wedding
I suspect of being planned for us
by the lizards. They plan to kidnap us
& take us to a lake, where they
will put us in a rowboat without oars
& leave us out there, together
until we marry ourselves.

It would probably work.
It would probably hold,
because our tongues are on fire,
how could we say a word?
Our arms are on fire, our lips are on fire,
our lakes are on fire & our fires are now lakes.
Hold my hand, I'll flood you.
I hold your hand, you flood me.

careful mtn by sour june monstr

I found an old bear in a box in the attic,
next to a macrame wall-hanging
my mother made when she was
pregnant with me.
I pulled him out, he was dusty,
& I scratched his ears
& he & I, we danced to my favorite
record, one that was recorded by a small lake
with a voice like gentle thunder.
I heard a rumor she got her start
on Broadway, where they paid her
to stand offstage with a mic
& make the sound of gentle thunder,
like the right kind of rainstorm
that makes you want to carry a small deer in it
& kiss a certain spot between her ears
until your clothes are wetter than spring.

Dear bear, I wrapped you
a present in paper I made
of sewn-up petals
from 1000 speckled flowers.
I can't wait 'til you return
so I can see the look on your face
& the look on your skin
& the lake on your shirt
& hear the way it sloshes over when you laugh
like a tee ball team leaning
on an above-ground pool.

I've been letting my braids grow long
so that someday I might knit you a home
that will be here no matter what.
I have been hiding letters in it
for us to find later
that say wonderful things
about warm birds &
egg salad potlucks held
in fire-colored city parks
that happen to be shaped
like my favorite parts of your hair,

speckld flours

where all the smoke-drunk
wasps formed a committee
to discuss the terrifying mystery
of storm doors & window screens.

& some bright day,
when all our lakes' beaches
are thick with the right lizards,
maybe I will hold you to my chest
& tell you about the speckled flowers
I have been pressing in books.
All the dead plants
I've kept to show you.

careful mtn by sour june monstr

ix. - xxiv.

# WARM MORNING

I woke up & found this morning broken
into sixteen pieces & it shimmered around me
when I moved my eyes across it. I examined
the pieces one by one. It seemed like
the first sliver of morning was a river
to whom I had written a letter.
It went as follows:

Dear river, you are upon us.
We hid behind a ledge & you
threw yourself over it, sparkling.
Every part of us is made
of the thing that moves you.
We are forests that
forgot we were forests &
started kissing, pressing
our walnut trees so close they
would crack.

Dear river, meteors have been found in you.
You, ground! You, river! You, stream!
This has been done before,
but I'm doing it again,
because I thought it was beautiful.

Dear meteors, this is the sequel
to a movie that won Oscars
but this movie won't win any
Oscars because the love
interest has already played
the dad in too many Disney movies,
like the one where a middle-
schooler makes a million dollars
carving seahorses from rotting wood
& selling them as idols to cults
of younger middle-schoolers.

Dear love interest, I am holding you
hostage in a shoebox with
airholes to take to school under my coat.
Dear airholes, I am making 10000 of you like the stars
in this dream I had about
a star-ceiling'd church of cats
with holywater dishes
& those churchmice heroes
who fought valiantly for reformation.

Dear other forest,
I have collected 5000 seashells
I am making into a blanket for you
with gentle crimson thread &
sweet woodsmoke.
I want to see you wear it
over your head on some cold spring
Saturday we don't leave the house
& sing songs about mothers
into each other's mouths
until our tongues have fresh newborns
we can name Elijah 1 & Elijah 2
with hands like miniature bears,
the softest skin we've ever felt.

worm mrning

& when I looked at the second sliver
of morning, I had a dream about a version
of you with horse eyes, we were sitting
in a beautiful restraurant whose waiter
kept bringing us cakes. He came to us
with one last cake & told us
the restaurant is closing because
you ate every cake the kitchen staff
could make for the rest of their lives & so
you sprang for the check &
we walked down by the river &
looked out at the boats in the night.
Three boats were having trouble
getting up a waterfall & we helped,
because from where we were
standing they just fit on our fingertips.
They took turns thanking us &
gave you the magical power of
water & now my hand goes
through you unless it's cold out.

From there we walked to the park
& I told you about three words
I made up & you said the middle
one meant feeling made
out of roller-coasters on fire, like
every single thing was made out
of roller-coasters on fire, on fire
but still running, & when you
touch another thing or touch
your arm with your hand or
touch your fingers together the
roller-coasters crash & everyone
who wasn't burned up already dies &
they show footage of this on the
news all day & your parents
email you links & say isn't this horrible?
in the subject line.

When you told me this it made me
swell up with love for you & I
remember thinking
I am a wasp for you.
I am this swollen-up wasp for you & we
are held here together in a dream that
could only hope to contain what we feel.

You took a seat on a bench &
told me that the last word—of the words
I made up—meant walking through
the shampoo aisle at Walgreen's
& overhearing someone
whose face you can't see
say to another someone
I just can't take it anymore.

worm mrning

When I looked again I noticed that
the third piece of morning was sitting
not far away from me & had its toes
in the cool garden dirt outside
our window. It pulled a seed pod
from its stem & broke it open.

Inside there was a smaller you
& a smaller me with all our arms
in slings, kissing like we were
in another dream I had, one
where you were directing
a play about loneliness & I flashed
the stage lights so they spelled
out I love you in morse code & then
the whole audience rushed the stage
& kissed the actors until their jaws
were sore & a tornado peeled the roof
off the theater & took you away
& I smashed the lights with my hand
until I really knew what your play
was all about.

The smaller us came & sat on our
window sill & tapped on the glass
with their tiny teeth & nails & we
opened it up & held them in our hands
saying you are so, so small.

careful mtn by sour june monstr

When I looked for the fourth
piece of morning I couldn't seem
to find it until I realized
it was actually this song you
had stuck in your head for weeks &
that I know this because you installed
a zipper & opened your head up
in the back & the most beautiful
sounds came out. The zipper's teeth
looked like the fir trees along I-94
north on the way to your parents' house
the time we were singing Silver Springs
at the top of our lungs to keep away
the slippery gray sky that had been
holding us between its teeth like grapes
& I zipped you back up & gave you a
kiss that I hoped meant I need you to hold me
like a small bird born too early.

worm mrning

Next, I immediately found the fifth
piece of morning, which was one where
we entered our apartment for the first time
after a long time away & when we opened
the door we slowly realized we had entered
a movie set made exactly to look
like our apartment. The props
staff had done a remarkable job
finding the small brass cat figurine
with just the right level of tarnish,
but the dimensions were all off
in some way we couldn't name.
Wardrobe handed me a dress
that was exactly like the one I
was wearing, but in a minutely
shifted shade of pink & the floral
print somewhat smaller.
They handed you a white t-shirt &
cute shorts just like the ones you were
wearing but you didn't need a belt
with these, didn't have to keep
pulling them up & the shirt had
a picture of a mother & baby fox,
the two of whom had moved just
slightly from how they had been
screened before.

I turned on the bath to find the hot
& cold had been switched
& as I undressed, our two small
cats now jumped eagerly into the
water, playing in it the way we had rolled
& kissed in the ocean days before.

As I laid back in the tub I looked
up to see that the ceiling was
now painted with clouds & then the
cinematographer tilted a camera

up to reveal a different ceiling, filled
with live horseshoe crabs mating
in the dim light coming through
our windows.

In the pocket of your shorts you found
a lottery ticket with a note written
in a loose scrawl on the back,
the lines curving wildly up &
down the little rectangle.
You read them aloud with some
difficulty, backed by the sound
of the soft clicks of
horseshoe crab shells moving
against one another. It said
In god's presence it is
possible to always be happy.

This all very quickly bled into the
sixth morning-piece, where I rearranged all
of the furniture in our apartment to
spell out the future of our lives
together. It was long & by
the end I had written us into
a corner & was mostly using the
hair ties & cat toys I found under
the wardrobe. Mostly it said you
are beautiful / mostly it said I love
you / mostly it was like the smell of
apples / mostly it said can we
get a dog for me to watch lie
across our legs when I wake up at
six & don't know whether to sleep
another hour or make coffee
that will be cold before you yawn
out your name for me like it is a question
against the worry that people in raccoon-
shaped masks pointed at me with thumb
& index finger pistols & took me far away
from the warm valley I keep
next to your warm valley
all night in our bed.

This last sliver left me exhausted
& I tried to go back to sleep, but couldn't
keep myself from looking around to other
morning-parts. I saw so many then, almost all
at once, but I will try to list them here separately.

The seventh was tiny,
& looked like a barrel
of light going over a waterfall
that froze halfway down,
& reminded me of how
I read in the news
about the girl that got stuck
on top of the ferris wheel
& filled her mouth with clouds.
When she got down birds flew
straight through her.
She rained the bed every night
& in an interview her mother
talked about how she began
to worry & decided to break
the lock to the girl's diary,
which was full of love
letters or suicide notes
written in glued-down wasp legs
she had been coughing up in her sleep.
It mentioned the time she had
cut open a D battery with
bolt cutters from the shed,
just to see what was inside,
& burned her face so badly
that no one looked at her anymore.
It was at this moment her mother
realized that after all this time
she did not know what her
daughter even looked like.

The eighth piece of morning was a long
picket fence I had written a letter to.
The letter was on pink scented paper
with sweet stickers of cartoon animals
& it said Dear long picket fence,
I realize this is a bit unusual
but I wanted to take the chance to let you
know how important this job is to me.

I spent all my money on
fields to lie in, & I have forgotten
to brush my teeth for years.
I want you to know that
I am highly qualified for something
I don't remember, but I assure you,
long picket fence, it will be valuable
some bright spring day
when we've all cleaned our glasses
& are done with our studies
& have exactly the right feelings
for this interminable bear market.

Long picket fence, I have long
admired your crosspieces
& while I am not made of wood
I think I would thrive
in such a position.
I know my first impression is a thick one,
but deep down I have long white
bones that could be tied tight &
straight. They could be an asset
to your fine team.
Thank you long picket fence,
for your consideration.
I am a fan of you, & the great
work you do & will continue to be
until the day I can no longer stand up,
due to how my legs seem to be

###### worm mrning

getting thinner than can hold
my heavy top parts.

This next piece, the ninth, came quickly,
& was a single blood orchid
in a vase of blue marbles
that the sun came through
like a swat team yelling out,
Everybody on the ground!
We are your mother & we care for you!

& it's true!
All the family photos, all this time they were
there for me & I cried there on the floor,
thinking of them in labor in the back seat
of my dad's Nissan, probably the only time
in his life he broke the speed limit, & my
tears became lakes & I spent hours sitting
on their beaches, trying to make out
their far shores in the foggy cold.

Their voices I can barely hear now,
& all my 4-H projects are about crying,
but I win all the ribbons
& the judges leave the country
to write soft bossa nova songs
about foxes that are metaphors
for the way the sun looks at 6pm
over the tree line in late May &
the swat team helps me with my rent,
just until I can get back on my feet,
& I give them my love,
& say I'll pay them back,
but I never pay them back.

Swat team, I miss you
please keep me in your hearts
& please mention me still
in the letters you write to your friends
who have been abroad
so very long now.

| | | | | |   worm mrning

Give them this handkerchief
embroidered all over with the words
cherry blossoms. It was sewn for me
by my dearest, oldest friend, who was
talented, soft-hearted & overly literal.
Whose sister I had to hold so tightly
at his funeral when she was shaking
too hard to stand.

careful mtn by sour june monstr

I took a short nap & upon waking
couldn't stop looking at the tenth
piece of morning. I spent what felt like
a long time in it. I remember that it had bright
green insect wings & that you were there
& that we were both strong sea-gods
who knew what it felt like to sit
in wind that was taller than the trees
& know that we were pushing it.
I kissed you in the rain & knew
the rain was only there
because I wanted to know
what it felt like to kiss you in it.

& I vowed to bury my face in you
& bury all of our clothes in the yard
beneath the tree by the fence
& you said we will dress only in sheets,
& thick crowns we crochet
from the soft hair we are growing
on the new limb that we share.

The eleventh morning-piece was harder.
In it you were mowing the lawn drunk
in mid-December & you told me I was the prettiest
delirium tremen you'd ever seen in the snow.
I used my hallucinated finger to draw a picture there of a
future you & in its eyes you said you could see such quiet confidence
& financial solvency & memories of the soft encouragements
you sang to our new, brittle children while they slept.
Your tears froze on your face & I picked them off
one by one & held them in my mouth of snow.
Because in this morning I'm not real but just
a thing you can put your hand through.
But still you came
& picked me up,
& held me there
& hoarsely croaked
I love yous as I bled water
all through your white sweats.

Ten birds were on the ledge outside my window
(I guess this was the twelfth little shard of morning)
& three of them took turns attacking
the others, who seemed impossibly
oblivious. It was raining & somewhere
inside a song was playing.
It was a song about a starving goat
& the girl who raised it,
who petted it every day &
fed it small rocks &
in the chorus the girl told the goat
she would never love anything
more than she loved it,
her perfect little goat.
& this refrain repeated,
beautifully sung over trembling
strings as the birds finished off
the last of their group,
devouring it into their beaks
& I banged on the glass
& tried to open the window
which had been painted shut
long before I was born.

I wanted at this point to get out of bed,
to make the rest of the day happen already,
but the thirteenth little sliver of this warm
morning was there in front of me,
keeping me here. I'll tell you about it now,
since we're here together.

This morning was a rock in the mouth
of a cave I came across fly fishing.
It had a word written on it I couldn't
figure out, except that it made my mouth
move something like azimuth or coriolis
or some other word I couldn't hold all at once
& I said it softly while inhaling,
like an apartment fire you keep
in your chest when your town is too dark.

The fish I caught were scaleless & sang
I'm Still in Love with You like a choir
you hold in a box next to your ear
for comfort when you can't make yourself
leave the house. It was beautiful & I sat
listening to it there in the cave, while they
twitched on the ground all around me.
Then the fish-altos lit matches all at once, in unison
& that cave lit up like a bronze statue caught
in a floodlight, revealing all our parents,
who were there with knives in their teeth,
looking hard at me & they asked where you were
& I said you were in surgery
& they asked what was wrong
& I said you were in surgery
& they said no,
what was wrong that you needed surgery
& I explained how the doctors don't know
how it got there but on the x-ray there is a
tiny not-you that is just like you but dead
& it is growing & pushing the you-you out

& they have to act fast or there will only be
not-you, this dead-you left in you & the fish started
crying & their matches went out & I was alone there
saying the word on that rock again & again
like it was your name, like I was a nurse
in the wrong waiting room.

|||||  worm mrning

Almost done, I found
the fourteenth shard of morning
on the wall above my bed.
It looked like my favorite picture of us.
In it, you are 2 years
old & I am the ocean
& you are building a sand-
castle on my beach.

Later that day, your mother
pulled you out of me, crying
& found a jellyfish wrapped entirely
around your fat little leg.
Shortly after this picture was taken
your sandcastle gained legs &
a meerschaum pipe it smoked wolves in &
I have to say you put incredible detail into
the wolf-teeth for a sand-artist so young.
Next to it you built a tiny sand-house
that looked like a beautiful marriage
& sat on the coast of a sand-lake
shaped like a pile of 1000 grenades
with the pins pulled, & it was stocked full of
rainbow trout & blue gill & mermaid
& a slow glance you gave me that
felt like the end of everything.

The glance grew up near a decayed
boot & its mother was a strong woman
who was good at impossible sea-math & underwater
rocketry & the boot did a solid job as a father
figure & the glance got accepted to a fine
college attended mostly by blue gill & a few
pregnant mermaids with whom it became closer
than it ever had been with anyone
& a few of them remain its closest friends to this day.

For your glance's fifth wedding anniversary, they chipped in
for a marvelous glass sculpture of footage
of a bear destroying a Whole Foods, a gift it likes to share
a cigarette with on these new warm nights we've been
walking in like they have always belonged to our skin.

Next to the fourteenth morning-part
hung the fifteenth part of morning,
which looked like a fallen
angel. I mended her wings &
kept her in a shoebox with air-
holes & fed her drops of
yogurt & celery pieces until
one day the shoebox was empty
& there was a note left behind.

The note said that I had helped her greatly,
but her god was a jealous god
& she was sorry for what was
about to happen. It said I was
a machine that could be broken
& I had parts I couldn't see,
parts that could be held in a wrench
& twisted hard & her language
slipped off the page somewhere
while describing the effects
of what I was about to experience,
like meaning was something you
could just take scissors to.

I folded the note until it was the
size of a quarter & took the filet
knife from the kitchen. I cut a deep
slit in my thigh & buried the note
& sewed it shut with dental floss
& prayed to her god to grant me
the ability to know where he stopped
& I began.

careful mtn by sour june monstr

It was probably afternoon by the time I came to
the sixteenth piece, the last piece of this morning.
This one looked like a sad blanket made
of my opinions on things. It wasn't warm &
you shivered so hard under it that it looked like
you were being shaken by a strong man intent
on letting you know the building was on fire.
The building was not on fire but I pretended it was
& pretended to try & put it out & pretended
to put water on everything & pretended to escape
except I couldn't because the pretend ceiling
had fallen in in the next room & our pretend
door was barricaded shut & I was inhaling
so much pretend smoke & my pretend shirt
was on fire & so I laid down & rolled
on the ground until I pretended to pass out
& pretended to die next to you, still asleep in bed.
Our whole families had pretend funerals for both
of us where they pretended to cry & pretended
to say nice things about how they would pretend
to miss us. Once we were in the pretend ground
I finally woke you up for real & said we are finally
alone & you got this look on your face like 1000
suns in 1000 skies. We pretended to dig
ourselves out & eloped to pretend France where
we had a pretend goat farm with real goats that
gave us looks like we didn't know what we were doing.

The farm was a success & was soon made into
a major motion picture that no one saw & three
sequels that everyone did see but no one liked.
In the third sequel a beautiful Hollywood actress
played you & you played me & I played the part
of an injured goat & our parents were played by
sunsets who had gotten their start doing Shakespeare
somewhere. It ended with a magnificent shot of the both
of us dragged by a team of horses across the pretend French
countryside until our faces were covered with

dirt & blood & we were grinning from ear to ear
& holding each other & kissing our necks as our heads
banged against rock after rock after rock after rock.

The soundtrack was full of wistful piano music,
a song from which I tried to play at your real funeral,
fifty years later, but couldn't make it through.
Your parents were gone, but the sunsets came
& told me it would be okay, & I made the mistake
of believing them.

xxv. - lxxvi.

TO JUNIPER,
WHOM I LOVE,
& the
AVALANCHE LIGHT
SHE MAKES ON THE GROUND

*Dear love interest,*

I apologize for the coded nature of this message.
The amount of work you must have done
to transcribe this letter into what you are currently
reading is laudable & for this I laud you.
You are a beekeeper, an avalanche &
it has recently become very important for me
to tell you something you already know, or
could have easily guessed.
I want to tell you something about bees.
I want to tell you something about how when I was 10
my class went on a field trip to a factory
where we learned about how jobs were made
from processing rain clouds, from separating
their silver skin & pushing their gray parts
into pockets we don't have to live in yet
& how my teacher started crying apparently
because she was pregnant & then we had to leave early
& eat our lunches on the bus. Love interest, maybe
you remember, because I think you were on that bus too
& gave me your yogurt & pressed it to my leg & said
look how it's still cold & we threw away our brown sacks
but you kept your spoon & made it pretend
to work at the factory & made it pretend
to be so happy, with its salary & benefits
& short commute & it stood on my arm
& led a union meeting there
& you said I think it likes you.
Maybe you don't remember,
but the roof of the bus peeled off then
& we laid down in the aisle
& watched the clouds
going into the factory.

Love interest, did we even go home that day?
Because I remember us lying there
pointing out the shapes of the clouds
& telling each other what they were doing
& I wonder if that stopped, or if maybe
you are just describing to me
a me-shaped cloud
that is writing this letter
to a cloud shaped like love interest.

Where do you keep your bees?
Last time I saw you, I went looking for them
& all I found was old tires that had been chopped up
& put into hives & told to act busy. They were
remarkably sculpted & trained, but
the smell gave them away.

Write me another letter in a code
so deep I can put it in my mouth
& never really know what it means for sure
& that will have to do, that will be best for you
& for me & for the bees, wherever it
is they & their ghosts have run off to these days.
I am carving a picture of you with a dragon
on a mirror in a Starbucks bathroom.
I hope you get it, & I hope it finds you well.

Love always,
Sara

to junipr, whom i love

Dear Juniper,

We have not spoken in nearly
a year. You are an apartment fire.
These past months have held me thick
& heavy, but recently I have felt a spark.
I feel like a dog in the rain.
I feel very left on a beach.

All of which, of course, has me
thinking of you. Do you remember last summer,
when we planted lit fireworks?
& they turned into lit firework trees?
They have begun blossoming again, unexploded
as ever. I used their leaves for tea &
accidentally prophesied an air raid.
You probably read about it in the paper.
Fourteen planes got caught in the too-thick
clouds above our town & started dropping bombs,
but the bombs just thudded down on the
pavement by the riverwalk.

I guess they weren't really bombs.
I guess they were bowling balls. I guess
they had these love letters written on them
from the pilots. I guess they were all in love
with the same woman. I guess her skin
is like the feeling you get when you find
a long piece of hair that isn't yours
under your shirt, the way it tickles
as you pull it out.

It reminded me of me & you,
of that time we piled in your car &
drove until the interstate gave out &
we

careful mtn by sour june monstr

pulled over & I took off my shirt & you
drew the stars on my back so we could
figure out later how to navigate
back to the exact time & place when
the recorded world was set on fire.

I heard on the radio that some scientists
have taught themselves to deeply
believe that all possible things are always
happening at any given moment in another
dimension & it makes me feel good to know
there is an earth where we are still sitting
on the hood of your car, which
you have named Rachel,
& maybe humans have evolved
to produce spider silk & we have woven
a blanket to keep us warm while we fall asleep
& the air is as sweet as licorice.

Everything came down after that.
I don't want to talk about it &
I know you don't want to hear it but
everything came down after that.
June, these are the things we've got.
& now I've written a letter about it &
I don't have to look at it & you do
& that's not fair.

I've attached some photos. I want you
to have them. They've been haunting me
& I am tired of feeling like I'm living
under swords. You're stronger.
So here. You have this.

All the best,
Sara

to junipr, whom i love

## Avalanches.

When the sun pushed out morning, I was carrying you
in my teeth. I was a she-wolf & you
were my cub & I didn't know
how to tell you that I didn't care

when you set the kitchen floor on fire & when you
complained about how small your teeth
are I only opened my mouth
to show you how small mine are too.

Cub! Avalanche! Let's put our combined wardrobe
in a MegaBus bathroom & talk to how big the sky is here.
Dear how big the sky is here, we don't have the words!
Some of our wolf-clothes are getting wet & a song
exists to tell us exactly where to put our eyes
when there are slim wars standing outside
our idling cars holding roses.

& please tell your mother you are always in a church,
one where the walls keep shifting & the songs have thick
bass & the clergy understand that we both want to die
& come back as 2 sleepy pups. Now the choir
all makes bonfires on the roof with pew wood
& now we put 3 lizards in the basket
as a prayer request & now there is a tiny sign
at the foot of our bed with our Latin names & the countries
where we can still be found in the wild.

Dear same thing as before! Let me hold you after service
like our fathers held each other before those wars came in
in their beat-up coats & stroked our braids & rubbed
the soreness from these old wolf legs. & please!
Please promise you will cling to me just like that
when a Denny's waitress is drowning
 an eagle in a river
                & you are the Denny's waitress
                & you are the eagle
                & you are the river.

Dear Juniper,

I can fully appreciate you
without lying awake singing you broken
over & over in my head tonight,
but you seem to have different ideas.
Maybe I am wrong.
I am willing to consider that possibility.

I haven't seen you since you left
to visit your aunt who was dying of poetry.
You jumped on that bus after the night
we watched the pink dolphins
hovering over Lake Michigan
when the sliver moon's circle
was as big as our tiny fists
held at arm's length,
& now when I think about it
I can't remember which parts of you
I made up & that's okay.
Everything is so full right now &
I am running out of containers
to put things in.
The real last time I saw you
was today when I turned your
labradorite necklace & you were so
blue & green at me.

For now I am a barely spinning
coin I need someone to put their
finger down on & this night's
temperature is a lizard moving
in my hand I might drop.
Juniper, stay with me on this,
because I'm either onto something

||||| to junipr, whom i love

or else I've finally found out what our
endpoints look like & they are beautiful
& just shy of what I imagine
a mother can't ever seem to say
about the crying thing
that just came out of her.
But as you well know,
that's just guessing on my part.

I know the blood all over you means
you have a noisy heat that's always
sizzling off in the too-cold,
but I can never really seem to figure out
what the blood all over me means.
Give me just a few more animals to hold,
because honestly right now I feel like I
won't even believe in winter again
until it gets here.
Like, maybe if you can wash the
clouds around my hands
I can wash the
clouds around yours
& if nothing else I think the next
best thing to keeping promises
is getting better at making them.

Love always,
Sara

careful mtn by sour june monstr

Dear Jupiter,

I am worried I may have written you by mistake
on one of these nights where it looks like god
has just started making things up.
Last week the wind blew all day for a week, long,
long after we were sure the sky
would surely have run out of breath.
I'm not sure who you are, but a man
in white loafers told me once to tell you
I love you but I'm not sure if that's meant
to come from me or him.

I've been carrying a bag of rocks
around in my coat just in case
the storm comes to get me again.
Last time it was a red storm full of
animals I made up for drawings when I was tiny
but this time I'm worried they'll have real
fur & teeth where the scribbles went.
I've been buying new cigarettes lately that
don't like fire & when I try to light them they
just squirm off into the holes I've been making.
Did I mention I've been making holes?
Does it matter?

I read how there's a documentary
about 2 people who were in love
& I have a suspicion the first one
might be some mutual relative of ours
& that the second one might be made
of the feeling I get when I wake up
before my alarm & everything is still
shivering in the too-bright our apartment
sometimes has.

Keep well,
Sara

to junipr, whom i love

Dear Juniper,

I keep trying to put the time our eyes
locked together back into the present but
somehow it is on a separate mesa from me & the gorge
is filled with different parts of weird donkeys &
my hands aren't touching things right anymore.
I just want to make sure we look
the same still, or like a version of some resurrectable thing
I might still see tonight if I were to go
outside at this late hour, which I know I won't.

Juniper, the math just doesn't work out. When
can we live like we're always about to get on
an airplane? As it is we keep holding
hands with ourselves like there isn't a
word for love, but there is &
it's so easy to spell.

I tried to send you the last
letter I wrote you, but it was returned
with all kinds of extra stamps I didn't
put there originally & it smelled like a
vitamin store. If the lake goes under we're
all going down with it & that's just how
things are, right? Yesterday I bought 50
feet of chicken wire & today I returned 50
feet of chicken wire. I think I'm just spinning
my wheels until you make the stars
turn back to the colors they were
when I was in grade school & you
weren't even a thing to speak of.

Or maybe you're older. What I mean is that
we used to be able to conquer worlds like touching
a little anthill & now it feels like we've
charted the gaps inside of us to the point
that it's obvious where the darts
would go. Just tell me it's impossible for someone
to stop being invincible later on after starting out that way.

I'm just spitballing here but what if
we cleaned our glasses? Maybe there
are some careful mountains out there that aren't
on fire, but are just smoking a bit.
No, wait, Juniper, forget all that, because I want to set everything
we do to organ music & put red velvet on all the floors.
You know, we could lay in the grass & touch our teeth to rocks.
I'll sell my car & burn the money in our hot air balloon torch & you
can drop out of school to read tarot. We'll roll the sleeves on our
t-shirts up a little bit & kiss in front of people we haven't met,
Juniper! There are too many sandboxes to push our hands in
for us to be this out of it & that's wrong. I'm tired
of pushing against my boundaries like there isn't light
slipping in from everywhere all the time & those cracks
are us-shaped. If I can touch the skin on the back
of your hand & move it I'll light every lamp in your hair &
that's a real promise.

Love,
Sara

to junipr, whom i love

Dear bad guys,

This is the last letter I will write
to you. This morning I left too early
for the train, so I am giving you
these minutes I have as the sun
puts its shirt on.

You are all anchormen, but it's like
you don't even know where to put
your anchors down anymore.
Why is this?
Lately people have been pointing
out the woodfire I have burning
in my chest & I suspect it has something
to do with you. I'm seeing you
everywhere lately but your limps & slings &
that horrible cough all make me
think you might be about to pray
away all the death on your clothes.

& is there any way you could cry
more often in general but less
often directly outside our bedroom
window when we are sleeping?
When I get the window up
in the morning I have to say hi
to the water you made there,
though obviously you've
hightailed it by then. It has been
leering & spitting at me lately &
to put it flatly I don't like it.
More on this later.

Also, just as a thought

careful mtn by sour june monstr

experiment what it would be like if you melted
down those anchors you've got &
made fresh, proud boats both to keep
in the sound & to sail out of it.
Dawn's too cold for me now, &
the shaking I do wakes the deer
up, so you can have it. I think
you'll be more than impressed
with their silence & colors.
This is all for now.
Please write.

[I never know how to close
letters to people I don't like anymore.]


Sincerely,
Sara

Dear Juniper,

Have I lost you by now?
We haven't written in a handful &
I am wondering if I ever really knew you
or if my letters are underneath some snow
somewhere. It's winter now, a cold one,
& last time I saw you there was sun, or warm
rain & that could mean months or years or
lives ago, but I know once on one of these
days we made clouds with our breaths mixing
& washed our faces & grew braids long enough
to feed the winter birds from. I grew 5 braids
& you grew 12, I think, maybe my numbers
are off though, but I know your skin was spotted
then, & mine was striped, & moved across
my back when the sun was out.

Were you a season? Or a dragon? Or a river? Probably
all three, knowing you. It's time for my bath now,
but let me know when the marble
teeth I carved you finally wear out,
because I can always make more
& the ones they sell in stores
don't have the love mine do.

Please write,
Sara

*You are an avalanche washing my feet with your avalanche hair.*

You are an avalanche washing
my feet with your avalanche hair & all
I can do is press my lips to your back & whisper
the new name I made up for foxes.

I counted off the time out loud & a waterfall
started over us from the river that had been living
in the kitchen cabinet with all our
bowls & mugs & your face was the sun & my feet
got cleaner & cleaner.

You looked up at me & opened
your mouth & 30 brown dogs
fell out of it, tails aloft, looking for their mothers. I told them she
was you, you this avalanche with your dark avalanche hair
& you took them in & gave them coffee
& pastries from the secret stash you kept beneath the kitchen
island, which was an actual island
whose churchgoing population
once said prayers in our names,
but now regards us more
gingerly, like parents
who have gotten too old
& repeat themselves too often
to be feared.

The river took the dogs & their coffee into town & to church
where they did such terrible things things I won't write here,
thinking the clergy would be scandalized,
but no one was scandalized, because we all live in this world
together.

& so we came

|||||  to junipr, whom i love

& picked them up                in your avalanche car
& we didn't say a word, but the dogs         were whining
& the river leaked through    the seat & we all traded skins
& I was a dog
& you were a god
& I wanted to be you
& you wanted                to be the sky that night
& the sky                   that night wanted to go home
& get some rest, because the    stars had gotten too heavy to hold
& so I looked in my pocket
& pulled out this rain so thick that we
            could all get lost in it together
& then you weren't anything
& I wasn't anything & the sky
                                        wasn't anything
& the dogs weren't                anything
& the lawn wasn't         anything but wet & good
& glad to be these new, rare beasts.

Dear thing I am going to call the world for now,

What is your name?
How do I know who I am talking to.
I am writing you this to tell you
about the feelings I've been having, how
they hold little flags & spell words in
semaphore & how I don't know semaphore
but I got a book from the library & how it had
baby vom on it & how I felt like that was
probably close to what my feelings
were saying in the first place.

Have you ever been conquered & if so
what does it feel like? Does it feel like
when you drive through the woods?
Does it feel like small movements?
Does it feel like the sound of
Stevie's voice in Landslide?
Is it a whole thing that contains itself?

In the letter I wrote you before I said
You're prettier without statues of angels on you.
It was a weird letter because it was shaped like
a very handsome dog we once had
whose legs were so strong &
made us think of how we
might be able to abolish fear
from our lives with careful attention.
It was shaped something like the world.
Something like you, but crying.

There is a faucet somewhere &
you can turn it on & love comes out.
There is a toilet you can sit down on

to junipr, whom i love

& love comes out.
There is a kettle you can use
to make morning coffee
& when it heats up,
love comes out.
Give me a torch to hold while I'm
sitting through the parts of work
that make me want to pull up the carpet
& lie underneath it & go to sleep crying
while watching a movie where
everyone dies in the end.

World, that is not a movie I want to watch
but that is a movie I totally want to watch.
The Christmas presents I am giving you
are made out of sound
& will make you hold your breath
until love comes out.
When you smash the right piggy banks
you can fit the pieces back together
so it looks like the world
& through every crack,
no matter how much rubber cement
you dump in there,
love comes out.

We are growing a plant I am naming Samuel
& the taller it gets the more I will know
just how leaves can make a sound
that sounds like the chorus
when we sing it naked, skin glowing
here on our blanket in the dim starlight.

Blow in my hair & I
will blow in your mouth

& we will see what happens
when the world works.

Love,
your daughter,
Sara

Dear Juniper,

There is a woman sitting
next to me who has a
glacier inside her. She says
she didn't know it was there
until it started to melt.
She says it's going
to take years.
She says
I am less numb
but it hurts more.

She cries sometimes,
at night, & her tears
are colder than anything
I have ever felt.
It is shocking to touch one.
My whole hand spasms.
The ceiling here is wood
sloped like the inside
of a roof & I can feel
my eyes roll down it
toward the walls.

The woman sitting next to me
is a painter & there is a pile
of things she has painted
during her time here.
These are watercolors she made
from the makeup in her bag,
of blooming shapes outlined
into clear thingness.
This is all a process, she tells me.

In the morning
sometimes the woman
will change clothes before
she thinks I am awake
& I see her & I think she is
beautiful but I know she does not
understand her own beauty.
In the afternoon I tell her
this & she says so what.
Let's say I am beautiful,
she says. What then?

The night here is cold
& I wonder about her glacier.
I wonder what canyons
or mountains it has made.

Love,
Sara

Dear Juniper,

It was great to hear from you again.
We see each other all the time, I know,
but it's always like someone handed me
a freshly cut watermelon I wasn't expecting.
You are beautiful, & I am a girl
with a name like a state park
or something else with boundaries
that are just made up.

What are your arms doing right now?
Are you holding them like this, like I am
holding mine right now, like I held them
on the day we came home & the whole
apartment was filled wall-to-wall with pink
balloons & we just popped our way to bed?
Remember how we didn't even bother
with the other ones, how we were so tired,
& so we slept for a few lifetimes & woke
up as presidents? I was the president of
smoking or some other thing I don't really do
anymore & you were the president of the tiny
lizards we used to find out crawling by the dumpster.

Is there something spiritual in making
more intentional fashion decisions
or am I making this up?
I mean I am making this up
but am I right?
I mean if I told you I was
a dragon or a cloud full
of birds you can't see
or a bear in a forest
who just ate the whole forest

but regrets it, would you believe me
or would the whole world I've got,
or at least the parts I trust carefully,
come down crushing like the weak
ceiling above your friend's
friend's bassinet?

The thread my house is hanging by
could pop any second & bring this whole
taco joint with it & you & everyone
are all made of scissors lately.
When did that happen?
When did crying all the time get so dang cool?
When did this parking lot fill up with cars
that are about things? Was I not paying attention?
Because this car is about dying &
that car is about what people say
to themselves in the shower &
that car is about how much I love
you when your hair is wet.

Your friend talks too rough sometimes
& I'm a photograph of the sound you just
made when I told you about dogs driving but
I still have to haul this suitcase full of water
to a new location. People like drugs
because they're the closest
to magic but real magic exists it just
doesn't care about what we want,
& I don't blame it. I'm just a parked car somewhere.
I'm just one of these closets in a room full
of closets but I'm all painted shut
so just trust me when I say there's
a whole lot of nice ponies hanging
out even if you can't get to them

to junipr, whom i love

to scruffle their ears.

We don't think the sun is too strong
in wintertime but it's just far away
& that's how I feel right now,
like I'm driving this truck with
broom handles connected to
broom handles & I'm out
sitting on the tailgate, trying
to keep my hair in place.
I just want to see what happens
when it finds its own length.

Love like always,
Sara

Dear understandable thing,

I understand. You are soft & clean,
& my hands are so dirty
from touching tires all day,
from my job as a tire-toucher.
I received a message for you
by accident. It is enclosed.
Though I didn't read it
I assume it is from a lover,
from some whirlwind affair
you once had, possibly
with a whirlwind.

I assume she says something
about how she feels like she
can understand you, & perhaps
something about the way the
abandoned newspapers hang
on the upper deck of the commuter
train in the earliest morning,
when the businessmen have
seats enough to nap in.
I assume it's full of songs
without words that make you feel
like a taxi who doesn't know
how to get home, driving in the
desert with his meter on
just to see how high
the numbers go.

Lemon-scented,
I'm wearing real boots &
my teeth can hurt my tongue
if I push down hard.

to junipr, whom i love

My mother grew tomatoes
& I grow tomatoes.
I can't judge you &
neither can god,
whom I've talked to & she
is just as sad as all of us
but more & don't
believe anyone who tells
you otherwise. Just as sad
as the bugs you keep.
For your tomatoes.

I'm a realizer, & I realize
you are old now, much
much older than when
You started reading this,
but before I go, I want you
to know that I forgive you completely
for everything that happened
that summer my nose bled
from the top of the slide
& you kept all the bark chips
All the bark chips there were.

Love,
Sara

Dear thing that is trembling in the cold dark not late but early,

Hold my hand when my face
wants to cry but only yawns.

Hold my head when all sound comes
into focus as one sharp buzz &
the world makes a decision about
how blurry it wants to be & that
decision is very.

Lick my wounds & put me on a shelf
next to a candle for a ghost of heat
that can come tell me how cold it will be
once he's leaned away again.

Drive me to the bus stop & see me off
to sleep in a seat until I can arrive
in a place that will whisper at my sadness,

Come out lil guy.
It's okay now, everyone is gone,
left for work you're not doing

& my dreams will still be a place
with rooms about everything
except what has come to crush me.

In your name,
Sara

Dear Juniper,

We have to keep taking pictures
of the sky so we know
what she's been up to.
This heavy-legged
loneliness I've been wearing
for the last little while seems
to be going & transition
implies that at some point
you achieve the state
you were headed toward.

You put your fingers in my
hair so often these days
that I can never fully forget
the feeling or how soft
your skin looks when
your shirt rides up.

I am the girl you saw carrying
her bike up the front steps
with the lights still flashing
against the trees & you
are the feeling I have
when I finally sit down.
You are conversation
that comes in tides
just slow enough
to forget everything perfectly.

All my love,
Sara

Dear Juniper,

Two women are building a house
around a dying animal.
They go to the river
& dig up clay
to make into bricks
they bake in an oven.

The bricks stack up high.
Four, five deep.
The walls are thick.
They leave space for a window.
They leave space for a door.

They finish the house
& the animal says
thank you so much,
but I am still dying.

Love,
Sara

Dear Drapes,

I admire the confidence with which
you are wearing that floral.
Bravo. You look fantastic.
But you are in a room I can't quite figure out.
The first time I came here
there was an ox with a massive
head wound, lying on his
side & I said hi.†

He was bleeding all over the floor
& it was really getting everywhere.
I tried to step around it to see his face.
I bent over to shake his hoof
(which he did not even lift
for me to shake) & noticed
him looking down my dress.
I'm sure you've been there, drapes
because, in that moment I was trying
to figure out if things
were about to get horrible
or sexy & if the difference was
perspective maybe? for some
people? it never was for me.
I mean sure, he has a cute head
wound but really, drapes,
all I was thinking was I
didn't ask for this.

But drapes, we had an alright
time of it. Or at least
alright enough to make
Me want to come back
now that the ox has gone.

I didn't get that job, drapes!
But maybe we can make
our own jobs from toothpicks
& pipe cleaners. Maybe we can
clean pipes.

You can start with mine, honestly,
They've been dirty forever &
I've been too shy, & too busy trying
to tie a piece of my hair to this fly
to make him a fly leash
so I could take him on flies
around the apartment
like a wingy dog or a
super chill cat maybe.
& maybe just maybe
if you get my pipes clean enough
I could get a real wingy
dog one day. You could move in,
or I could, & we could just
have a dog together.

We could sit different places
around the apartment together
& you could tell me about
why I'm sorry all the time
& what it is I'm sorry for.
You could tell me the story
about when you were a kid
& your older sister picked you up
by your ankles, how your dress
fell down over your face
& about the neighborhood kids
who told you your sister
was a jerk for doing that.

to junipr, whom i love

How they were trying to make you
feel better but you defended her.
How you didn't get that you could
switch alliances occasionally,
& like everyone just enough
but not fully.

Don't ever tell me how much
you like me, drapes.
Don't ever tell me you're in love
no matter how many times I tell
you that I am. Because the thing
of it is, the real thing is that
I don't ever want you to have to take
it back, or even, eventually,
come to understand that
other plants, or even ideas of plants,
sometimes come in & put down
roots deeper than I can,
after mine have bottomed out.
Drapes, I love you for
your strong confidence
& fashion sense,
& how you don't
ever look up at the stars
when we're out sitting on the porch
& I've asked you a question
that means too much to answer.

There's some vodka in the freezer,
feel free to use it when you get home,
for anything at all.

Yours,
Sara

†

[Hi, said the ox, looking up. We received your resume, he said, you seem plenty qualified but we wanted to meet you in person, he said. We wanted to meet you in person to make sure you have what we need. What do you need, I asked him. We need a key to the bathroom, He said, gasping for words. The head wound looked like it really hurt. We haven't been able to get into the bathroom for weeks, He said. We really have to go badly. We didn't see anything on your resume, He said, about a key. You've been holding it for weeks? I said. Holding what? He asked me. I guess I don't know, I said.]

Dear mouth opening into a yawn,

Why did you disappear so quickly?
After our time together I was hoping
we could really make something of this
something lasting more than a few
soft bars to hum later over train sounds.
My wheels are fully greased for once
& all I've got to lose are these shapes
I've drawn in the snow, one looks like
a duck, & that's nothing.
I don't need a duck.

I tried to photograph your soft lip stretch
but failed to capture the beauty of
its gentle song & dolphins are smart,
sure, but in what way? & what does it
mean to us? & how do we know
a tree isn't smart? Or a rock? Or a
smile?

Mouthgesture, you're a real beauty,
a total knockout in fact, I just don't
have real teeth anymore, it's all
synthetic in here & the sun has
words for that kind of thing,
right? Fire-words? That can
keep us warm & kill us all at once?

This thing you're telling me is the real
live dog I'm holding right now, or
it's what he looked like as a scrappy
pup, still suckling. Hand me a few
candles for the road & I'll belt out
something fresh & cool that looks

like the time you turned around
& I wasn't there all of a sudden.

Where did I go? You never figured it
out. You just went home & hung your
newest paintings, still wet, & the leaves
outside said soft things, those little
hey-we're-wet-toos.

Keep well,
Sara

to junipr, whom i love

*Dear tiny lizard woman who is a feeling I have about the way the world could be on the days I let myself step outside the wrong-shaped church I live in, into this new place & its endlessly diffuse sunlight, which is incidentally perfect for photos,*

Hey. I found you in my garden.
I mean I guess it's not my garden
really, it's just a place outside
the house I'm borrowing a tiny corner
of from a singer, just for this week.
I love the scales you have & the ones you don't,
the ones you gave up for lent &
how the dirt gets in the gaps they left &
how the parishioners kicked you out when you
left them in the offering plate with a nickel
you had to carry there with your toothlessness.

They kicked you out because you're too small &
the record label said the same when
you went in & gave them yr hot new track
the one you recorded when the singer was out
with the microphone he would have let you use
if you just had the words to ask.
Lizard woman I would publish your song!
& I would write you a sonnet if I could
ever seem to make the words fit,
but in the mean time here's this sprawly thing.

I mean I like you, lizard, & as one lady
who doesn't look like a lady to another,
I think we should plan some sort of picnic here,
a cool one we can eat cheaply at & wear
these dresses I found in the drainwater
outside the actress's apartment
where she lives with her sister,

careful mtn by sour june monstr

who walks dogs for a living
& maybe I'm wrong but
I think that would be a cool job?
At least for a little bit?

Oh, I'll wash them, sure, but I'm pretty
sure the wax they've got on their fronts is
a fashion choice, or at least we can figure out
facial expressions to wear them with
that will make others assume so, right?

The dance I'm doing
looks like the time I
pulled into the garage at 16
& mixed up the gas & the break.
It looks the way the door to the kitchen
looked after & like the look on
my dad's face then. But your dance!
I love yours. Yours looks like the idea
of guardian angels if we keep god
out of it. Like magic moms
with wings who like to turn
off our ovens just because.

I don't know if I believe in that
but what of it? I've got yr dance
& the way the sun looks here
& all the cool new flowers
that can't live back home,
the same way I couldn't live there.
Sometimes you can't seem to put down
any roots without the frost coming in,
but at least I can dig my own
new dirt holes. At least
I'm good at that now.

|||||  to junipr, whom i love

Keep well lady & I'll see you
around when the rain comes,
which is a lot more often out here
& a lot easier to dress for.

Love lots,
Sara

Dear thing that is not a thing but maybe a hole,

You are pushing me to my limits &
I have to say I don't like it one bit.
There is a song I forgot all the words to that
maybe I could be singing but I'm holding
too many rocks to really focus right now.
In the morning today there was a
killed dog on the fence just left
here like furniture & I get the feeling
I'm a dress you once wore
or a heat scarred piece of brass
you kept on a string around your neck
after the doctors found it inside you.
Christ-child, you dance to a tempo
way too slow for me to keep up
& I'm light enough I just
blow along the beach
off to who knows where.

Why couldn't I come back this time
as a sound that came out of you
instead of this clunky lost thing that
can't seem to figure out which parts
of her make sense & which are
going to cause more trouble
than they are worth for all of us
& are there other things here too
like when I was 8 & thought that if
I was going to live my life as an intelligent,
curious person I had to look closely at plants
& find something there worth memorizing.
It's like the sun's already come up
but I don't have the windows to see it
& there is a deer outside gently

## to junipr, whom i love

nuzzling my house & her
scratches match the timing
of the sounds of the gun battles
in me & there are gun battles in me
& maybe you two have met before.

I used to have all these
cops in my pockets until you
moved in & now I must have dropped
them all somewhere & I guess that's ok
but what next. Let me live here in peace
or somewhere else in peace or at least
let me know how locks work inside
if I'm going to be out locksmithing.

Drive me to a sunset but let the air
be warm enough for some nightcrawlers
to keep me company. I have been told
you drive a hard bargain & that's fine
but these worms & me have to know what
the hell it is you want or we're going to start
throwing some dirt already.

Until the rain comes,
Sara

Dear Juniper,

This dirt I have
in my pockets is a promise
about wings we had & lost.
How many muscles does a person
forget how to use over the course
of a calendar year?
How many does she remember?
Is this a constant?
In this warm light, do
my feet look like women
who braid their hair only
when the sun is coming up,
& have easy dances for children?
Because I would like them to,
but today the wind is too soft
to think straight.
I want to build a house with holes
in the floor that go down to places
they have old myths for.
Ones we've read & others
that are probably lost
to wherever our wings went.

I don't miss them really.
I miss all kinds of things:
one specific dog, the smell
of people's hands, something
I remembered when I was a kid
& forgot everything about except
for that moment of remembering,
the girl with the pet egg
whose brother broke it
& how when she cried

||||| to junipr, whom i love

her parents wrote overtired
on her hand in ballpoint pen.
How I kept a pet egg for weeks after,
swaddled in my electric blanket
until its insides dried up hard
& rattled when it shifted.

But I don't miss wings,
maybe because they
had holes like my house
that guests had to step over.
A dream is a place you go
to let things happen to you
& you are a place I go
when I am a girl
& a mountain
& a beach no one's been to
to see it's sunsets
& feel the way
they almost seem
to touch your skin.

Yrs,
Sara

Sara June Woods has published under many names, most recently Moss Angel. She is author of six books, including Sara or the Existence of Fire, Sea-Witch v.1 May She Lay Us Waste, Sea-Witch v.2 Girldirt Angelfog and Sea-Witch v.3 Mare Piss Superkill. She currently lives in a black house in Olympia, WA with her wife and two rodents. http://undying.club

www.ingramcontent.com/pod-product-compliance
Lightning Source LLC
Chambersburg PA
CBHW071747080526
44588CB00013B/2177